CHAKRAS

The Definitive Handbook On Activating And
Harmonizing Your Intrinsic Positive Energy Through The
Methodology Of Chakra Purification

Maxime Rivest

TABLE OF CONTENT

Balancing Of The Chakras 1

Attaining Equilibrium In Life: The Ultimate Objective 9

Guiding The Prana 23

The Manipura Chakra For Regulation 43

Using Energy Healing Methods 80

Restoring Equilibrium To The Throat Chakra 100

Meditation And Yoga 127

Balancing Of The Chakras

The methodology for establishing equilibrium in your chakras is relatively straightforward and does not necessitate extensive time investment or unwavering dedication. In recent times, there has been a significant body of literature dedicated to exploring the concept of achieving a harmonious equilibrium between work and personal life. This global literary endeavor aims to promote consciousness and understanding regarding the importance of maintaining a healthy lifestyle. The aforementioned principle applies to the harmonization of chakras, as it encompasses an intricate procedure that primarily involves determining your life's priorities and assigning appropriate importance to each of them. Encountering individuals who prioritize either their professional pursuits or their personal lives to a significant extent is a common occurrence, and it often proves to be disadvantageous for many of them. This is due to their belief in the utmost significance of establishing a successful profession, thereby enabling their family to partake in a comfortable standard of living. However, in their relentless pursuit of career advancement, they inadvertently overlook the needs of their family. Similarly, there are those who place a great emphasis on prioritizing their family, ultimately resulting in a compromised professional trajectory and, subsequently, strained familial relationships. The alignment of chakras is comparable to the harmonious equilibrium between one's personal life and professional commitments. As previously outlined, there is no inherent spiritual or religious connotation attached to it. Rather, it is a therapeutic method that has gained recognition and endorsement from contemporary medical experts, akin to the acceptance of yoga. What are the methods for achieving chakra equilibrium? For achieving the appropriate alignment of chakras, individuals ought to meticulously assess the various facets of their life and identify those areas which require attention and improvement. Subsequently, it would be advisable for him to cross-validate them with his chakras, as previously indicated. It is imperative to adhere to a regular routine of performing this practice to ensure that any instances of imbalance are promptly recognized and addressed. Take heed of your engagement with the natural world, the allocation of time dedicated to your loved ones, and the extent to which you allocate it towards socializing and forging new acquaintances. Monitor your dietary regimen and physical fitness activities. Examine the artistic facets of your character and the manner in which you articulate your thoughts and concepts. Furthermore, it is imperative to maintain a comprehensive log of instances wherein you selflessly provide assistance to fellow individuals, occasions during which you allocate your thoughts towards the preservation of nature, and moments wherein you conscientiously focus on the intangible facets of existence. In the event that these options prove insufficient, you may opt to compile a comprehensive schedule of respective pursuits aligned with each of the aforementioned seven chakras, while diligently noting the duration allocated to each endeavor. When formulating your list of planned activities, it is advised to allocate a designated segment for documenting the duration you devote to each individual undertaking on a daily, weekly, and monthly basis. By referring to this table, you will attain a definitive mathematical outcome that shall aid you in discerning various facets of your personality. You will gain a clear understanding of your priorities, major concerns, and the activities that prominently shape your life. Based on these findings, an assessment can be made regarding whether it is necessary to distribute one's efforts and time across multiple tasks, or if it is more advisable to concentrate on a few specific areas that are currently receiving insufficient attention. You are required to formulate a comprehensive strategy that allocates appropriate attention, in accordance with their respective priorities, to every aspect of your life. Should you neglect to do so, you will come to realize that you are lacking in the essential requisites of existence. What is the process for implementing the necessary modifications? When you are aware of the specific areas where you may be either overemphasizing or underemphasizing, it becomes necessary to make appropriate adjustments. Nonetheless, it is expected that your modifications should not be excessively sudden and assertive. It is essential that you implement these changes gradually and consistently to minimize any adverse impact on your well-being. If attempted, implementing significant changes within a limited time frame may prove arduous and yield proportionately limited benefits. As human beings, we require a certain amount of time to relinquish our former habits and embrace new ones. In the event of recognizing an excessive workload, it is recommended to gradually diminish the daily duration dedicated to work. Make an effort to allocate some time to engage in casual conversation or engage in a rejuvenating walk along a designated path. Try socializing with people. Enroll in a meditation or yoga program. Similarly, should your life revolve around prioritizing your family while neglecting self-care, I suggest immersing yourself in a new skill, such as acquiring fluency in a foreign language or honing your calligraphy abilities, among others. The crucial aspect is to commence with one facet and gradually enhance it initially, before proceeding to the subsequent one, so as to cultivate a state of harmony within your existence. Through persistent dedication, you will swiftly begin to witness a substantial affirmative influence on both your mental and physical well-being. Furthermore, this phenomenon engenders an augmentation in levels of contentment, as the state of one's physical, mental, and emotional well-being is intricately connected to the subjective experience of happiness.

Attaining Equilibrium In Life: The Ultimate Objective

Naturally, akin to a majority of metaphysical systems, attaining equilibrium in one's life is the ultimate objective. Engaging in meditation or cultivating mindfulness serves as an auspicious starting point for addressing these energies, albeit it should by no means be considered the final culmination of your endeavors.

External behaviors can likewise contribute to the harmonization of your chakras. Apologizing for a mistake, regardless of acceptance, is an act of equilibrium. The act of returning borrowed items, settling debts, and meeting obligations can also be described as actions aimed at achieving equilibrium. Engaging in acts of altruism, bestowing one's generosity, and fostering affection towards individuals or endeavors are proactive endeavors that emit a transformative force; in order to attain equilibrium, it is imperative to embrace reciprocating gestures - they can manifest as a mere smile or a pleasant sensation- in the form of receiving love and channeling energy.

The water cycle serves as a notable instance of a reciprocal system that underpins the existence of all life forms on our planet. Precipitation descends from the atmosphere, replenishing bodies of water such as streams and oceans, before undergoing evaporation and ascending once more to the clouds. Subsequently, these clouds condense, resulting in the downward return of rain.

The Chakra system functions in a similar manner. The root structure functions in a manner that simultaneously transports and draws energy, propelling the lower energies upwards across all the centers. In a similar vein, the crown chakra facilitates the descent of higher energies, directing them downwards through all the centers until they reach the root chakra, where they are pushed into the earth, subsequently prompting the upward retrieval of earth energy.

When all the centers attain equilibrium, meditation and mindfulness serve as effective methods to achieve such balance. Consequently, this cycle ensures the individual remains rejuvenated both mentally and physically. When one experiences equilibrium and vitality, the harmonization of other aspects of life becomes significantly more attainable.

5

The Fourth Chakra

The Anahata represents the fourth Chakra out of the seven in the human body. It is located centrally within the thorax, precisely upon the vertebral column in close proximity to the cardiac region. The Heart Chakra is situated centrally among the remaining six chakras. It maintains equilibrium between the material (lower Chakras) and ethereal (upper Chakras) realms. Furthermore, it exhibits connections with the respiratory system, integumentary system, and displays associations with the thymus gland within the endocrine system. This particular Heart Chakra pertains to matters relating to affection and compassion. However, caution is necessary. This should not solely revolve around your own interests. It is imperative that one does not prioritize personal ego. The desire for love is not the focal point. Rather, the Heart Chakra pertains to the act of bestowing and spreading love.

A well-functioning Heart Chakra is distinguished by attributes such as empathy, tranquility, inner peace, equilibrium, and sound judgement.

Grief is indicative of an obstructed Anahata. If an individual has encountered a situation of loss, they are likely to experience feelings of distress and unhappiness. It is imperative for you to acknowledge and come to terms with your defeat. Expose all of your sorrows in your immediate vicinity. You have indeed experienced a profound sense of bereavement, however, love constitutes a type of kinetic force that permeates our surroundings. When a cherished individual departs from our midst, it is solely their corporeal vessel that has departed from this earthly plane. The affection that persisted between yourself and the deceased remains present. It has not departed from this world. It holds paramount significance within the depths of your heart. The affection shall be rejuvenated through the emergence of a distinct form of love. Do not oppress yourself with overwhelming sorrow. Let go of your sorrow and grief entirely. Allow the pain to dissipate.

Additional indications of an imbalanced Heart Chakra include timidity, seclusion, dearth of compassion, incapability to absolve, relational challenges, emotional distress, maltreatment, and marital infidelity. Should your Heart Chakra display excessive dominance, you may find yourself relying excessively on others for acceptance and gratification. From a physical standpoint, it can manifest as cardiovascular and respiratory ailments such as asthma and pneumonia.

In the event of experiencing solitude and a lack of affection, redirect your cognitive energy towards an individual or entity worthy of devotion. It is not a prerequisite to possess shared humanity. It is not mandatory to share common humanity. It is not obligatory to be a fellow human being. There are numerous alternative objects of admiration, including flora and fauna. When one's Heart Chakra is obstructed and experiencing distress, it is beneficial to direct one's affection towards the botanical kingdom, arboreal entities, and fauna. Please proceed with the adoption of a pet or the establishment of a garden. Foster and cherish it. Feel free to embrace a tree if that is your preference. However, it is imperative that you always remember to harbor self-love. Should you experience an emotion and choose to suppress it, this will equally impact the equilibrium of the chakras. In order to liberate your Anahata, it is imperative to articulate your sentiments or demonstrate emotional openness. When expressing your disappointment with someone, refrain from withholding your emotions, while maintaining a composed demeanor and avoiding overt displays of anger. Kindly articulate your sentiments in a polite manner. After concluding your experience with that particular emotion, release it. One should never overly attach oneself to an emotion. As you progress through the contents of this book, it becomes apparent that attachment is not a favorable attribute. To maintain the optimal health and unobstructed flow of the chakras, it is advisable to refrain from forming deep attachments to both negative and positive emotions. One alternative way to unlock your Anahata is through cultivating the ability to embrace and acknowledge. Once more, the crux of the matter lies in the presence of attachment. If no further action can be taken in regard to a matter, it is advisable to disregard it. In the absence of alternative options, it is necessary to acknowledge and accept the circumstances presented.

Meditation, similar to the practice employed for the other Chakras, proves efficacious in facilitating the unblocking of the Anahata. Please rest your hand upon your chest while in a state of stillness, or alternatively, direct your attention solely towards your heart. Imagine a green energy light slowly getting bigger until it occupies your wholeness. One may also envision the act of bestowing and receiving love without conditions. While engaging in the mentioned activity, vocalize the phonetic representation "YAM". Your assertions could be "I am receptive to forming emotional connections." I am in association with other individuals. I harbor a profound appreciation for the aesthetic allure of the natural world and the diverse realm of fauna. I harbor profound and unconditional affection for myself, coupled with a genuine acceptance of who I am."

In the practice of Kundalini yoga, the process of purifying the Heart Chakra can be facilitated through the performance of asanas (physical poses), pranayamas (breathing exercises), and the repetition of mantras, known as ajapa japa.

The Sacral Chakra (Swadhishthana)

This pertains to the second chakra, specifically situated slightly below the navel at a distance of approximately two inches downward. Evoking the essence of the color orange, it is intricately connected to our inherent sense of childlike wonder, artistic expression, and uninhibited impulsivity. The sacral chakra pertains to our capacity for establishing connections and embracing unfamiliar encounters in our existence. It addresses the dynamics of interpersonal connections, human sexuality, the ability to understand and share the feelings of others, as well as the experiences of joy and opposition. The emblem of this entity takes the form of an inverted crescent, and its designated precious stone is the amethyst. It is correlated with the celestial body known as Mercury and interconnected with the faculty of taste. The sacred chakra is symbolized by the spiral pair known as the third eye, and its corresponding elemental representation is that of water.

The sacral chakra is associated with cultivating various types of relationships, which contribute to enhancing an individual's self-esteem internally and fostering an external understanding of sexuality, interpersonal connections, personal identity, and familial bonds. When your sacral chakra is unblocked, you become more receptive to forming intimate connections, exhibiting deep passion, and embracing the vibrancy of life. You do not exhibit any abnormalities or irregularities in your sexual functioning or orientation. Individuals exhibiting manipulative tendencies, a strong inclination towards control, and an insatiable appetite for lust showcase an excess of energy in the sacral chakra. Individuals with these characteristics also tend to exhibit heightened emotional reactivity and may demonstrate an intense preoccupation with sexual thoughts. Moreover, they display addictive tendencies that can lead to an almost cult-like influence. It is also prevalent in individuals with diverse dependencies.

Conversely, individuals who exhibit a dependence on others, display a martyr mentality, or demonstrate submissiveness may exhibit a deficiency in the sacral chakra. This deficiency stems from the sacral chakra's pivotal role in governing one's self-esteem, self-assurance in their creative capabilities, and their aptitude for establishing open and meaningful connections with others.

Some physical manifestations and conditions linked to the sacral chakra encompass muscle spasms, lumbar rigidity, renal insufficiency, and altered bowel regularity. The sacral body parts encompass the kidneys, female reproductive organs, large intestines, and bladder. Typically, the sacral chakra serves as the focal point for the accumulation of sensual and sexual energy within one's body. It harnesses the potency of artistic expression, inventiveness, and the faculty of the mind.

Guiding The Prana

The Manipura Chakra, also known as the Solar Plexus Chakra, is situated superior to our umbilicus. The vital energy necessary for sustaining life is directed towards the digestive organs through the consumption of food, inhalation of air, and intake of water. Should the energy flow be positive, it will result in a resilient constitution and the presence of optimum well-being. Consequently, this imbues us with a feeling of tranquility and assurance, as our cognitive faculties are unclouded. We acquire the psychological and affective fortitude necessary to transcend the adverse aspects that often impede our spiritual advancement. Through the transmutation of emotional energy within this specific chakra, we guarantee the unimpeded circulation of vital life force, known as prana, to the remaining chakras. We are encompassed by a sense of overall wellness, which exerts a favorable influence on our physical, mental, and emotional state.

In essence, our dietary choices determine our overall well-being. It is indispensable that we provide our body with nourishing sustenance prepared in a hygienic and serene environment. Consequently, we are capable of living vigorous and energetic lives. Conversely, should the body fail to efficiently assimilate the energy derived from food, we experience a profound sensation of weariness and tend to exhibit irritability. We are experiencing a state of perplexity and find ourselves incapable of adequately articulating our thoughts and emotions to external parties. Our apprehensions concerning rejection, ridicule, loss, mortality, and more. All of these occurrences stem from the obstruction of the Manipura chakra.

Over a duration, this could potentially present itself as psychological or physiological issues.

The Manipura chakra presents us with a valuable opportunity to surmount all our fears, negative habits, or undesirable qualities. Directing the movement of this energy and harnessing it to surmount obstacles that impede us will avert its unintended diversion towards the emotional and cognitive faculties, potentially inducing discomfort and distress.

Useful Practices:

The act of offering a prayer prior to consuming our meal results in the transmutation of the energetic essence contained within the food. This generates a state of harmonious resonance within the Manipura Chakra.

The mantra connected to the Manipura chakra is the sound 'RAM'. The resonations initiated by the recitation of this mantra instill within us a profound sensation of warmth and facilitate the unhindered circulation of prana, the vital force that sustains life. Reciting the sacred syllable OM or OM SHANTI serves to induce relaxation, instilling within us a profound state of serenity and self-assurance.

The hue that is connected with this particular chakra is yellow. This color represents illumination and possesses the ability to cleanse the atmosphere in its vicinity. Amber, Citrine, and Topaz can be regarded as crystals that possess the ability to heal, activate, and cleanse this particular chakra.

In the course of our contemplative practices, it is imperative that we strive to direct our attention towards comprehending the underlying motivations behind our actions. We will effectively navigate through our feelings of pride or enhance our self-esteem to cultivate a well-rounded sense of confidence in our approach to life. An optimally balanced Manipura chakra facilitates the seamless circulation of prana, instilling within us profound serenity and profound joy.

There exist numerous exercises that stimulate and purify the Manipura Chakra. A few examples include Bhastrika pranayama, Ujjayi pranayama, Virasana, Vajrasana, Trikonasana, and Santulanasana.

Three: Supplementary Sources of Energy

Furthermore, apart from the Chakras, there exist an additional four regions of considerable energetic importance.

The Physical Body

The Aura

The Hara

The Spirit

The Physical Body

The term "Physical Body" denotes the complete manifestation of our corporeal existence. It encompasses all corporeal elements, ranging from the epidermis, tendons, and musculature, to the pliable tissues, vital organs, vasculature, gastrointestinal tract, reproductive system, and neural framework. It encompasses all the physical constituents of our being.

The Aura

The "Aura" refers to an energy field that can be perceived through sensory observation, albeit discernible only to individuals who have cultivated an awareness of their alignment with universal energy. This degree of transparency necessitates honing one's skills; only a limited number of individuals possess an innate openness that allows them to perceive auras without cultivating their spiritual sight. Instead of being perceived as a continuous field, the aura is observed as a chromatic mist encircling an individual.

The aura encompasses a fusion of the primary energies of the Chakras, permeating both the internal and external dimensions of the physical body and enveloping it in a vibrant energetic sphere. The majority of individuals have encountered instances where their aura has been touched by others; however, due to a lack of comprehension, such encounters are often not identified for what they truly are.

Consider the most recent instance wherein you entered your residence or professional environment and, despite experiencing serenity and contentment, inexplicably encountered feelings of anxiety, anger, or sorrow. This phenomenon occurs due to the gradual assimilation of energies from your surrounding environment into your aura.

This occurrence arises due to the fact that your aura is composed of the cosmological energies. Consequently, if you lack awareness of your aura, you will have inadvertently exposed yourself to the emotional influences of those in your vicinity. Similarly, your aura has the capacity to assimilate your emotions, thereby exerting an influence on those in your immediate vicinity. Their aura has become attuned to your emotional state, often without their conscious awareness of this phenomenon.

By acquiring the skill to regulate your internal prana, you will simultaneously be controlling your aura.

The Hara

The 'Hara' is located approximately two inches inward from the navel and serves as a conduit to access profound levels of energy. This portal presents an accessible pathway through which we can access and harness the energy contained within, facilitating the accomplishment of our objectives.

This energy serves as the fundamental essence of our internal fortitude, comprising untainted universal energy unblemished by societal constraints or emotional conditioning that might influence our own life force.

Through attaining a harmonious equilibrium of our personal life force energy, we gain the capacity to tap into the Hara whenever necessary. Similar to many other aspects, the utilization of the energy residing within the Hara is an area that lacks awareness amongst the majority of individuals. Regrettably, we fail to comprehend the significance of what we are observing, resulting in our obliviousness to the undeniable truth that each and every one of us has the ability to tap into this realm.

Reflect upon instances where you could have observed or become aware of an illustration of Hara energy being employed.

Elderly monks engaging in activities that would typically cause severe discomfort, yet they remain steadfast and upright without displaying any signs of distress. This phenomenon should not be mistaken for a mere illusion as it instead represents a deliberate utilization of Hara energy. Consider the anecdotes about a maternal figure who effortlessly raises a vehicle in order to rescue her child - it is notable that this individual would typically lack the requisite physical prowess to accomplish such a feat, yet accomplishes it nonetheless, subsequently remaining oblivious to the means by which it was accomplished. This phenomenon can be described as an involuntary manifestation of the vital life force known as Hara energy.

Similar to the aforementioned illustrations, each individual possesses the capacity to access the Hara, extracting energy through the gateway and directing it towards the desired destinations. In a manner akin to the monks, each one of us possesses the capacity to attain a level of consciousness where this is within our grasp.

Acquiring mastery over one's prana and regulating energy flow within the

Chakras necessitates dedicated training. Acquiring the skill to intentionally access the Hara requires a significant amount of additional training, but it is indeed achievable.

The Spirit

The spirit embodies the fundamental core of your being. It embodies all that you are and all that you have the potential to become. It refers to the version of yourself that exists beyond the limitations imposed by your physical form. The corporeal form serves as our means of experiencing life solely on a physical plane. The essence refers to our preexisting state prior to inhabiting this corporeal form, and what endures beyond the eventual decay and demise of the physical body.

The essence of our existence resides in the highest realm of our being, and it is indeed attainable to establish a profound connection with it. Certain individuals possess the capability to engage in astral projection, wherein the incorporeal essence emancipates itself from the confines of the corporeal realm. Regrettably, the majority of individuals, including those who possess the capacity for astral projection, find themselves incapable of establishing a genuine spiritual connection with the cosmos. In the pursuit of tapping into the energy of the prana, it is imperative to establish a deep connection with our spirit, which entails aligning ourselves with our authentic identity and embracing wholeheartedly our potential for growth and self-realization.

Contemporary existence imposes numerous ethical and societal limitations, complicating the task of relinquishing them to establish a connection with our intrinsic being. The rigors of everyday existence necessitate adherence to these rules, yet they encroach upon the liberty of our authentic beings.

The essence comprises solely of affection. Unconditional love, devoid of any conditions, manifesting as pure, unadulterated love for oneself and an unwavering love for others. Genuine love lacks any form of self-interest; it merely acknowledges veracity and embraces the entirety of one's own and others' positive and negative attributes.

The Chakra of Communication (Throat chakra)

This particular chakra is interconnected with the anatomical regions encompassing the neck, shoulders, arms, hands, as well as the thyroid and parathyroid glands.

This energy signifies our capacity for effective communication. When the energy flow in this chakra becomes obstructed, individuals may experience difficulties in articulating themselves and engaging in effective communication with others. Obstruction could potentially be associated with throat cancer and other grave medical conditions. Our physical well-being can be severely compromised when the circulation of this energy is disrupted. It is crucial to incorporate the practice of maintaining equilibrium and nurturing our chakras into our daily routine. This designated space allows us to authentically express our deepest truths.

Insufficient knowledge of our own truth may contribute to a state of ambiguity.

When an equilibrium is achieved within this chakra, we can establish a connection with our elevated essence and freely express our authentic truth. Effective communication plays a crucial role in our day-to-day existence, as it enables us to articulate and assert our sense of self through spoken expression. In the event of an obstruction in this chakra, one may experience a diminished capacity for active listening, accompanied by an inclination towards excessive verbosity. This indicates a pronounced deficiency in your ability to articulate effectively and express your thoughts with clarity. After achieving equilibrium, you will enhance your listening abilities and acquire proficiency in engaging in constructive communication. One facet of this chakra pertains to the articulation of oneself, which synergizes with the process of discovering one's true identity. When engaged in the act of creativity, we discover activities that bring us pleasure and provide a platform to express our distinct qualities, thus granting us a profound sense of individuality. Upon fully embracing all the unique aspects that contribute to your identity, you will cultivate a heightened awareness of your personal reality and consequently gain the assurance that accompanies this understanding. It is essential to bear in mind, in the process of cultivating a robust understanding of one's truth, to maintain a disposition of impartiality. Every individual possesses their own subjective reality, and one's unique identity will invariably diverge from that of others. Do not rigidly clasp onto your belief system to an extent where you are unwilling to grant others the liberty to hold their own personal beliefs. It is imperative to refrain from forming strong attachments to our belief systems, as these beliefs are prone to transformation through the course of our experiences.

Ways to balance

Work on communication

By diligently cultivating effective communication strategies and practicing emotional resilience, rather than succumbing to fear-based reactions, individuals can foster a profound self-awareness and embrace the liberating experience of authentic self-expression.

Gaining self-awareness through the medium of artistic expression. What is your area of expertise or field of interest that brings you great enthusiasm and dedication? What makes you unique? Engaging in artistic manifestation, whether through vocal performance or pursuing one's passions, has the potential to facilitate a return to one's true self.

The throat chakra, known as Vishuddha, can also be harmonized by practicing the yoga pose called supported shoulder stand, commonly referred to as salamba sarvangasana.

The Manipura Chakra For Regulation

The third chakra is commonly referred to as the solar plexus chakra. The objective of this endeavor is to facilitate individuals in attaining access to their internal source of authority. By means of this, individuals acquire self-discipline and cultivate self-restraint.

Situated in the inferior region of the abdominal area beneath the umbilicus, the third chakra symbolizes the cognitive aspect of the individual and their innate sense of jurisdiction. An individual commences the process of cultivating the third chakra during the period of fifteen to twenty-one years of age. Vision is the sensory faculty associated with this particular chakra. It is commonly linked to the region of the upper abdomen, encompassing vital organs like the liver, middle spine, kidneys, spleen, small intestines, adrenals, stomach, and the area extending from the umbilicus to the rib cage.

The solar plexus chakra assumes the responsibility of storing and conserving energy, subsequently allocating it to the higher chakras. Hence, it is imperative to ensure the sustenance of energy in this chakra. This will aid in rectifying the incongruity within the third eye, throat, and heart chakras.

Activating the Solar Plexus Chakra

Commence by positioning your hands before your abdominal region, specifically at a slight distance below the point where your solar plexus chakra is located. It is important to ensure that your fingers are directed in an outward direction.

Now, please interlace your fingers at the apex. Afterward, place one thumb on top of the other. It is imperative that you ensure your fingers are fully extended. Direct your attention to the solar plexus chakra and engage in the repetition of the mantra "RAM."

The Advantages of Maintaining a Well-Balanced Solar Plexus Chakra

Individuals who possess a state of equilibrium in their solar plexus chakras experience a pervasive sense of reassurance. They frequently exhibit adequate nutritional status. These individuals exhibit a high degree of versatility as well. They possess a sense of self-assurance and ease with themselves. The attainment of equilibrium in the solar plexus chakra facilitates the cultivation of unwavering judgment and determination.

The solar plexus chakra facilitates our ability to make optimal choices for ourselves. It imparts the principles of assertiveness to us.

The acquisition of intrinsic authority is gained by cultivating the capacity to discern between moral and immoral, particularly for our personal benefit. The third chakra facilitates the acquisition of cognitive reasoning skills for evaluation of matters. Additionally, we enhance our ability to effectively resolve complex challenges.

The Consequences of Excessive Energy in the Solar Plexus Chakra

An individual exhibiting excessive energy in their solar plexus chakra may demonstrate a proclivity for transforming minor issues into competitive situations. Individuals who possess an abundance of energy in their third chakra may exhibit a tendency to impose their will upon others.

The Phenomenon of Low-Level Energy Within the Solar Plexus Chakra

Individuals who possess a diminished energetic state within the solar plexus chakra commonly experience sentiments of remorse, particularly in instances where they decline a request. Frequently, they exhibit a deficiency in internal control.

If an individual's solar plexus chakra is functioning suboptimally, they may experience difficulties exerting control and exhibit diminished or absent self-esteem. This elucidates the experience of vulnerability. It has the potential to evoke feelings of anger and induce a sense of lethargy. You might also experience a sense of perceived threat. This could potentially lead to sensations of undernourishment. It may also lead to the development of a condition known as a nervous stomach.

An inharmonious state of the third chakra not only has psychological and emotional repercussions for an individual. Additionally, it can lead to various physiological ailments, namely diabetes, gastric ulcers, dyspepsia, pancreatitis, anorexia nervosa, bulimia, and gastrointestinal disorders.

Strategies for Optimal Restoration and Harmonization of the Solar Plexus Chakra

To attain equilibrium in the third chakra, it is imperative to give due consideration to the subsequent constituents. To begin with, this particular chakra is correlated with the hue of yellow. The triangle serves as its emblem and fire stands as its elemental representation.

Peppermint, ginger, turmeric, chamomile, fennel, and cumin are among the spices known to possess the ability to restore equilibrium to the third chakra. Some of the food items that are beneficial for this specific chakra include grains, granola, pasta, cereal, breads, flax seed, rice, and sunflower seeds.

The designated formula associated with the solar plexus chakra is the syllable RAM. It articulates the phoneme associated with the letter 'O'. In the realm of gemstones, amber, yellow jasper, tiger eye, citrine, and chrysoberyl are known to harmonize effectively with the solar plexus chakra.

The third chakra also exhibits a harmonious affinity with fragrant essential oils such as lemon, lavender, anise, and chamomile. Bach flower remedies, specifically hornbeam, impatiens, and scleranthus, possess the potential to produce remarkable effects on the activation and harmonization of your third chakra.

Set a Goal

Establishing an objective facilitates the process of mending and harmonizing this chakra. When establishing an objective, ensure that you dissect it into manageable stages. Additionally, it is beneficial to establish a predetermined schedule for accomplishing each individual task. Commence the execution of the plan. Please maintain consistency with the predetermined schedule until you successfully accomplish your objective. Please remember to partake in the festivities.

Wear Yellow

This particular hue influences the energy flow of the solar plexus chakra. Donning this garment will stimulate a deficient third chakra. Observe the effect of this color on your state of mind, specifically, the stimulation it induces.

Watch the Sunset

As previously stated, the sense of sight is attributed to this chakra's sensory function. Engaging in visual activities, such as observing the sunset or sunrise, would greatly benefit you.

The sun serves as a representation of potent energy. Furthermore, it possesses an identical hue to that of the third chakra. Observing the setting or rising of the sun is an exceptional means of reaffirming one's inherent internal strength.

Engage in the cultivation of your intuition.

Intuition can be described as an innate insight that aids in discerning the optimal choices for one's mental, physical, and spiritual well-being. It facilitates the discernment of moral correctness and incorrectness. Should you desire to restore and harmonize your solar plexus chakra, it is advisable to diligently cultivate and fortify your intuition in earnest.

One strategy for cultivating this intuitive ability involves creating a state of mental tranquility. Please allocate increased focus towards your intuition. Try acting on them. Acquire the ability to place trust in your intuition.

Go for Tea Time

Partaking in tea consumption is more beneficial for one's health compared to the act of consuming coffee. Indeed, tea possesses miraculous effects on the third chakra as well. Peppermint, ginger, and chamomile are among the teas that offer notable benefits. These teas are effective in soothing both the stomach and the nervous system. They substantiate their efficacy in the restoration of your hypoactive solar plexus chakra.

Execute the Seated Twist Asana in the context of Yoga.

The seated twist yoga pose can contribute to the restoration of equilibrium to this particular chakra. To execute this posture, commence by assuming a comfortable seated position on the floor. Next, proceed to elongate your lower limbs until they are fully extended in a straight position, situated parallel to your torso. Maintain contact of your right leg with the floor while proceeding to position your left leg in a crossed manner over the right. Next, position your right elbow in contact with your left knee. Afterward, proceed to rotate your torso while simultaneously stretching your left arm rearward.

This particular yoga asana offers advantageous effects. Furthermore, not only does it stimulate the activation of the third chakra, but it also induces a therapeutic massaging action on the internal organs, thereby facilitating the process of detoxification. In order to enhance the detoxification benefits of this yoga pose, it is recommended to consume a minimum of one glass of water following the completion of the exercise.

Rely on Affirmations

The solar plexus chakra represents one's internal sense of authority. In addition, affirmations serve as an effective method for fostering the development of inner authority. Please consider attempting one or various affirmations from the selection provided. I have faith in my own abilities" or "I possess inherent worthiness" or "I am confident in my discernment" or "I consistently make sound judgments.

As one proceeds to recite these affirmations, a noticeable augmentation in both self-assurance regarding one's authority and confidence in their personal capabilities should manifest. Through consistent dedication and effort, one should also gradually amass a reserve of potent energy stored within the third chakra.

Additional methods of restoring equilibrium to the solar plexus chakra encompass the act of decluttering and organizing your unruly wardrobe. It is advisable that you prioritize the completion of tasks that you may have postponed or neglected for an extended period of time. Select an item that you can feasibly complete. Otherwise, this will solely result in further exasperation. Pay attention to grooming. Additionally, please remember to maintain an upright posture while walking.

These recommendations are effective not only in enhancing the strength of your third chakra. They can also aid in enhancing and augmenting your capability, particularly in making beneficial judgements, particularly in relation to your well-being. Simultaneously, you bestow curative energy upon the higher chakras, thereby facilitating the rejuvenation or attainment of equilibrium in your holistic chakra energy matrix.

Five: The Celestial Bodies and the Alignment of Your Energy Centers

Just as each chakra is connected to an endocrine gland within the human body, each chakra is also associated with a planetary counterpart. There exists a set of ruling planets, each possessing distinct characteristics and a unique essence. The chakras exhibit analogous qualities as well. Frequently, the planets are employed with respect to your date and time of birth. The particular configuration of celestial bodies at the time of your birth can exert an influence and shape your individual character. This alignment and relationship are depicted in a natal chart. What is intriguing about your birth chart is that it not only provides insight into your cognitive, metaphysical, and corporeal facets, but it also depicts the influence exerted by the alignment of celestial bodies on your energy and chakras. Upon inhaling your inaugural breath, you assimilated the cosmic energy present in the Universe at that precise instant, thereby indelibly impacting each and every cell within your corporeal constitution. That stamp constitutes an enduring component of your individuality. The moment that ultimately shaped your being is also the moment that delineated your vocation. It is your duty to perpetually share that gift with the individuals in your vicinity as you progress through your entire lifetime.

A way to approach the conceptualization of your chakra system in relation to the planets is to perceive your chakra system as an embodiment of the solar system. You epitomize a "microcosm reflecting the macrocosm." Thus, you possess within yourself the entirety of the universal energy reserve. In order to provide you with a more comprehensive understanding of this interconnection and correlation, the subsequent delineates the chakras and their corresponding celestial bodies, along with their interdependencies.

Your Root Chakra

Furthermore referred to as your Mooladhara, the chakra situated at the fundament of your spinal column is governed by the celestial body known as Mars. Inextricably associated with the astrological sign Aries, this celestial body is intricately connected to qualities such as naiveté, affinity for the Earth, capacity for discernment, sagacity, bliss, and uncontaminated nature. Your behavior exhibits a resolute and sagacious nature, which is harmonious with the correct trajectory of your purpose. You possess a remarkable aptitude for consistently making sound choices. With tremendous fortitude and great efficacy, you demonstrate an impressive level of strength, rendered in a manner that is gentle and amicable. The energy derived from Mars, and subsequently, the energy associated with your Root chakra, is inherently instinctive, organic, and remarkably potent. You possess remarkable bravery and vitality, in addition to being highly physically adept. If this celestial body and energy center exert a potent influence on your being, you tend to exhibit a sense of childlike purity and a fervent appreciation for the process of exploring the essence of existence.

The planetary and chakra influence on your sexuality is intricately intertwined. In the event of planetary imbalance or adverse planetary influence, your sexual experiences may potentially become exceedingly intense. Furthermore, this energy is accountable for the functioning of your reproductive system and its related organs. Engaging in highly intense interactions and morally questionable conduct concerning these bodily organs can detrimentally affect their level of responsiveness. The more pronounced this congruence and lucidity within this core, the more intense one's sense of purity becomes. Furthermore, as the alignment grows stronger, one becomes increasingly empowered to live in accordance with their purpose and maintain their purity.

Your Sacral Chakra

Termed as the Swadisthana chakra, this particular energy center shares correlation with the celestial body known as Mercury. It is situated within the abdominal region, specifically the lower abdomen, and the astrological signs Virgo and Gemini are subject to the influence of Mercury. This particular chakra and celestial body bear the responsibility for the regulation of your digestive system. You initiate the breakdown of adipose tissue, facilitating the release of stored lipids into your system to be utilized as an energy source. This procedure is indispensable for the optimal functioning of your brain. As it facilitates cerebral vigor, it enhances cognitive aptitude conducive to comprehension and reflection. Creativity and an appreciation for aesthetics are likewise intertwined with this energy. The influential nature of Mercury can assist in identifying pragmatic solutions for a range of issues, characterized by their comprehensibility and wisdom. This phenomenon can be attributed to the profound insight and ingenuity residing within both this particular chakra and its celestial governing body.

Mercury is renowned for serving as a conduit between cognitive faculties, the corporeal vessel, and the essence of being. The unadulterated wisdom of the cosmos permeates your being through this specific point of entry. The domains of the natural sciences and the liberal arts emanate from this source. This is due to your aptitude for comprehending intricate concepts and resolving issues with clarity and ingenuity. If one possesses a significant degree of influence from Mercury, they tend to be highly introspective. Though this inclination proves advantageous in problem-solving, it can present challenges in interpersonal connections. You have a tendency to become easily vexed and irate. It is of great significance to restore equilibrium in the second chakra as a means to stabilize this cognitive state and the accompanying emotions. Persist in making decisions that are both lucid and sincere.

The Solar Plexus Chakra Present in Your System

Occasionally referred to as the Nabhi, this chakra is situated within the lower diaphragm or abdominal region. It is linked to the attributes of advancement, benevolence, ethicality, equilibrium, and contentment. Furthermore, it exhibits robust characteristics of self-acceptance as well as acceptance towards others. The aforementioned characteristics are equally applicable to its celestial ruler, Jupiter. This celestial body also presides over the astrological constellation, Sagittarius. The nature of this planet is helpful and generous, but it also can cause everything to be prosperous or increase. This can prove favorable when implemented in positive endeavors, yet presents difficulties as it amplifies negative aspects. Furthermore, it possesses a connotation of auspiciousness, thereby augmenting the likelihood of a favorable outcome. This notion holds particularly true when deliberating upon your financial matters, which bear a profound connection to both this chakra and celestial body. It caters to both your spiritual and mental welfare. When the presence of something positive in your life becomes evident, you develop gratitude for your current circumstances and exhibit a propensity to readily extend assistance to others who are experiencing difficulties. You possess an exceptionally magnanimous nature. Consequently, as one's fortune grows and prosperity accumulates, an inclination arises to generously distribute this abundance among others. You never experience concern regarding your provision; you possess the utmost confidence that the Universe will perpetually provide all the necessary support you require. You consistently display contentment with what is provided to you, devoid of any desire for additional resources.

Should your influence be compromised or unfavorable, you may experience a sense of uncertainty or a considerable lack of equilibrium. Your thought process has the potential to veer into extremism and fanaticism. Due to the intensification of this energy, an individual may exhibit tendencies towards authoritarianism and extremism. One could potentially incur substantial debt without careful consideration, all in pursuit of opulence and aesthetic perfection. Hence, maintaining equilibrium assumes utmost significance. The planet Jupiter governs your belief system, spirituality, integrity, and fairness. If you are bestowed with the constructive influence of this celestial body during your birth, it inherently manifests in your character as sincerity, uprightness, and ethical behavior. As one progresses in personal development, this influence is further amplified, thereby fostering a deeper alignment with one's virtues and promoting an expanded perception of justice. In addition, it is probable that you will persistently endeavor to enhance yourself and extend support and counsel to those in your vicinity, thereby enabling them to pursue self-improvement as well.

Your Heart Chakra

This particular chakra serves as the dwelling place for the essence of your being, a divine source of unadulterated, unreserved love. Hence, this chakra is correlated with sentiments of empathy, genuine affection, and unwavering self-assurance. Furthermore, it is a chakra associated with the state of detachment. Excellent parents are cultivated through the nurturing and harmonious activation of the Heart chakra. The celestial body that exercises influence over this anatomical region is Venus, which also governs the astrological constellations of Libra and Taurus. A positive and harmonious influence stemming from the qualities of Venus instills a sense of well-being in those who are in your presence. You have the ability to cultivate an atmosphere of beauty and equilibrium.

It is probable that if Venus is present in your natal chart, you possess an extraordinary level of physical attractiveness. This exquisite allure extends beyond mere outward appearance, for it resides within the depths of your being. Your demeanor and conduct are indicative, thereby manifesting your innate affection and self-assurance to others. You positively impact the lives of others by exemplifying a genuine and compassionate demeanor, thus facilitating personal growth and transformation. The greater the degree of openness exhibited by your Heart chakra, the stronger the level of connection you forge with your Soul. As your Heart becomes increasingly receptive, an ever-growing surge of unconditional love emanates outward, encompassing all that surrounds you. This affection subsequently ignites the sentiments within others, prompting them to unfasten the barriers guarding their emotions.

The Crown Chakra

Situated atop the cranium, precisely at the pinnacle of the head, the Crown Chakra is harmoniously aligned with the hue of purple. Nevertheless, there are individuals who hold the belief that this particular chakra aligns with the hue of white. You may choose either option that aligns with your preferences; however, the color of choice for this book and its teachings will be purple. This specific chakra is recognized as the seventh chakra out of the total of seven chakras.

The Crown Chakra is credited with facilitating individuals in the acquisition of wisdom, achieving harmony with the cosmos, and establishing a connection with the spiritual domain. In the event of an underactive state of this particular chakra, one might experience a sense of disengagement from spiritual matters and find oneself prone to making a series of imprudent choices. In instances of overactivity, individuals may experience a sense of detachment from reality, manifesting as a feeling of having their thoughts ungrounded and struggling to establish a tangible connection with their surroundings. Both of these symptoms are unfavorable, thus it is crucial that you restore balance to the chakra in order to remedy them. When it is operating at its peak efficiency, you will be capable of establishing a robust connection with the spiritual realm without losing your sense of firm grounding in your daily existence. In the event of excessive chakra activation, it is advisable to seek grounding techniques in order to restore a sense of groundedness and connection to the physical world. If it is experiencing reduced activity, it is advisable to engage in meditation and establish the intention of revitalizing your capacity to engage with the spiritual domain.

This particular chakra holds the role of regulating the cerebral functions, the pineal gland, the inherent biological rhythms, as well as the spinal cord. In the event of an imbalance, you may potentially encounter afflictions related to any of these aspects. Your pineal gland's functionality may be impaired, resulting in disturbances in sleep patterns such as insomnia or excessive sleep. Additionally, you may encounter discomfort in the spinal region, as well as symptoms such as cognitive impairment or persistent headaches. If you observe a multitude of these conditions or any single one that seems to endure and prove challenging to regulate, it may be advisable to contemplate the restoration and harmonization of your Crown Chakra. It is possible that an imbalance exists, leading to a deprivation of overall well-being in any of these domains.

Upon observation of a chakra diagram, it becomes apparent that the chakras are arranged in alignment with the hues of the spectrum commonly known as the rainbow. This information is of great value to be aware of, as it will aid you in recalling the correlation between specific colors and respective chakras. Please be reminded that the color red is located at the bottom, whereas purple can be found at the top. Each chakra possesses distinct hues, sentiments, conduct, and bodily organs affiliated with its existence. In the event of an underactive, overactive, or otherwise unbalanced state, one may encounter symptoms that are associated with the functions governed by the specific chakra in question. If you are encountering distinct symptoms, it may be advisable to reassess the chakras in order to ascertain the corresponding energy center that correlates with the location of your symptoms. Subsequently, you may engage in chakra-related practices to restore tranquility and unity within it, thus potentially mitigating various or all of your symptoms.

Using Energy Healing Methods

Energy Healing can be classified as a form of unconventional or complementary medicine. Despite the skepticism of conventional medical science, it is a factual reality that energy healing is effective. Throughout the course of several centuries, countless professionals have administered aid to numerous individuals, delivering solace and assistance to vast populations. Energy healers possess the capacity to facilitate the unblocking of your chakras upon detecting any obstructions.

The approach employed in this field diverges significantly from that of traditional Western medical science. Traditional remedies aim to address the manifestations of the ailment rather than targeting the underlying cause. In spite of its potential for addressing the root cause, there is a possibility that the underlying cause may not have been authentically addressed. At their most optimal, these remedies have the potential to address the root cause from a physiological vantage point.

Nevertheless, it is evident that we, as individuals, transcend the mere confines of our physical existence. Additionally, we must also address our intangible aspect.

It is imperative to maintain a receptive mindset and cultivate a spiritual comprehension that acknowledges our existence as humans extends beyond the realm of the physical. Hence, upon realization of this fact, it becomes evident that solely addressing the physical components of the human body will never suffice as a comprehensive or genuine resolution.

There exist numerous disorders that commence with certain forms of energetic disruption. Moreover, they have the potential to induce physical ailments. It is imperative to address these matters in a similar manner as one would tend to physical concerns, in order to achieve optimal well-being. Therefore, the holistic approach strives to address the physical, mental, and spiritual aspects in order to eradicate the illness entirely. This approach encompasses holistic care and seeks to effectively address internal illness.

Fortunately, we possess a variety of Energy Healing Techniques at our disposal. Among the techniques encompassed are acupuncture, Reiki, aromatherapy, chakra harmonization, astrological guidance, chromotherapy, crystal healing, mindful contemplation, reflexology, pranic therapy, auditory healing, and shiatsu.

7: Positive Affirmations

Maintaining a positive mindset is paramount when it comes to implementing crucial life strategies. By employing potent techniques of optimistic mindset, constructive declarations, and visual imagery, you shall be enabled to attain your desired objectives. Acquiring the competitive advantage and wielding personal influence will be facilitated. This has the potential to revolutionize your overall well-being, greatly enhance the quality of your life, and infuse it with the vigor and contentment it truly merits. Envision the exhilaration and exuberance that would encompass your mornings, should you awaken each day brimming with vitality, bliss, and anticipation. That's a powerful feeling.

Adopting a mindset rooted in optimism and regularly reaffirming positive thoughts will cultivate a constructive outlook. This is imperative for optimal health and achievement. You will observe that the transformation of failure into success will be facilitated. Furthermore, you will have the opportunity to elevate your achievements to an entirely new standard. This will effectively serve as the energy source you require.

What do positive affirmations entail? These are indeed concise affirmations that focus on particular subconscious convictions, aiming to counteract and supplant pessimistic thoughts with constructive beliefs.

This constitutes a form of "cognitive restructuring," wherein one endeavors to cleanse oneself of unfavorable convictions. By expressing positive affirmations, or constructive statements, you will effectively channel your concentration towards your intrinsic objectives. They will serve as a gentle prompt for introspection and guide your focus towards maintaining a positive mindset and aligning your aspirations.

Through embracing the belief that the positive affirmations hold validity, individuals can incite either a process of reappraisal or avoidance within their subconscious mind. It will facilitate the alignment of your subconscious mind with the perceived inner truth. The organization can mitigate the challenges at hand by leveraging its available resources without fully addressing certain tangible issues that may be of concern to you.

This phenomenon can be identified by the presence of intense aversive emotions experienced when articulating these positive affirmations. However, in the event that one is encountering a state of contentment and elation, the mind will inherently and reflexively perceive all thoughts as incontrovertibly truthful. If you experience this sensation, you will come to acknowledge that the affirmations are effectively fulfilling their purpose.

Six: The Principle of Attraction

This is the point at which the study of energy and the realms of physical and quantum science converge. The principle of the law of attraction can be succinctly conveyed as follows: Similar entities have a natural tendency to gravitate towards one another.

This law operates on a daily basis: when searching for a friend's blue car, one suddenly becomes aware of the abundance of blue cars in the vicinity. Alternatively, considering the correlation between thoughts of food and the subsequent heightened awareness of the aromas emanating from culinary preparations and confectioneries.

This principle also extends to the energies that capture your focus. In the event that your heart chakra is experiencing an imbalance, it can be remedied by contemplating instances that demonstrate your being cared for and cherished, such as receiving thoughtful cards, encountering a friendly smile from a stranger, or recalling a warm embrace from a friend. These reflections will facilitate the flow of energies towards the heart chakra, affirming your sense of being loved and fostering a shift in perspective from negativity to acknowledging the achievements of the day at hand.

Nevertheless, the same principle applies in reverse. An emphasis on the unfavorable aspects will elicit thoughts of further negativity in your mind, creating a cycle that proves challenging to disrupt. Certain issues among these are likely to be genuine concerns that require concentrated efforts to mitigate their impact on your daily existence. After devising a strategic blueprint, contemplate the anticipated outcomes once the plan has been effectively executed. Reclaim the optimistic perspective regarding the situation at hand, as well as in the broader context of your life.

The outcome in terms of energy is dictated by the thoughts that occupy your mind. When employed judiciously, this has the potential to infuse fervor into your endeavors and bolster the efficacy of your objectives.

Four: Achieving Equilibrium in the Chakras

When endeavoring to acquire knowledge about the harmonization of your Chakras, one might find themselves contemplating the methodology for achieving balance across all chakras, given that the reasons for doing so have already been elucidated to them. In this section, you will gain insights into the current state or condition of your chakras prior to commencing their healing process. Furthermore, you will acquire knowledge on the necessity of maintaining harmonious balance within your chakras. Upon completing the reading of this chapter, you will possess the ability to discern the occurrence of chakra imbalance within your being.

Allow us to commence by acquiring knowledge of the diverse states of the chakras.

Different conditions of the Chakra

It has been previously communicated to you that the chakras have been referred to as the ethereal mechanisms of existence, conveying the understanding that these chakras perpetually emanate luminosity. There will come a point in time when the luminosity of this light will gradually diminish and its intensity will have significantly declined. That is why it is imperative for you to possess a comprehensive awareness of the current state of the chakras, thereby circumventing any potential complications that may arise in the future. It is imperative that you possess a comprehensive understanding of the manner in which energy circulates within your physical being. If there happens to be an individual in your proximity who possesses the ability to discern Auras, they shall perceive the presence of energies enveloping you, exhibiting a swirling motion akin to that of a vortex. This swirling energy center is known as your chakra, and it can be located throughout seven distinct areas of your body. You will observe the presence of the vortex in both the anterior and posterior regions surrounding your chakras. This assertion does not hold true in the context of the crown chakra.

Comprehending the conditions of the chakra.

It is crucial to acquire a comprehensive comprehension of the various stages of the chakras due to their paramount significance. Understanding the states of the chakras is crucial in determining the appropriate healing technique to employ. In this segment, you will acquire the knowledge necessary to discern the distinct states of your chakras for the purpose of facilitating their healing.

The Open State

In the presence of a revered therapeutic environment, one will discover the ability to initiate the process of restoring their well-being. During this particular state, the chakras are receptive and able to acquire the necessary energy. When the chakra is in such a condition, one will observe the unimpeded circulation of energy, as it permeates from the chakra to the surroundings and subsequently returns to the chakra. In the hallowed and therapeutic realm, the openness of your chakras shall surpass their customary state. Prior to commencing the session aimed at restoring equilibrium to your chakras, it is imperative to first activate the chakras.

The Blocked State

It has been brought to your attention that the chakras consistently possess a swirling energy within them. This energy manifests as luminosity, and when the chakra becomes obstructed, the luminous motion would cease its proper rotation and initiate a counter-directional spin. When a blockage occurs in one chakra, a corresponding blockage will manifest in the other chakras. This is because there is a complete absence of energy circulation within the chakras. When engaging in the process of chakra healing, it becomes necessary to harness and utilize the inherent energy residing within each chakra for the purpose of restoring its balance and well-being.

The Sealed State

The chakras possess an enveloping layer that serves as a protective barrier. This is the element that guarantees the optimal functioning of all the chakras. In addition, they ascertain the adequacy of the chakra's energy levels and take cognizance of its potentiality to derive replenishment from the cosmos. Once you have completed the process of restoring harmony to your chakra system, it is essential to take measures to properly close or seal the chakras.

The Restoration and Harmonization of the Chakras

This is the condition of the chakra once it has undergone full healing. Once the healing process is complete, the chakras will attain a state of equilibrium, rendering them equal in size. There will be a sufficient amount of energy present in the chakras during this period, as they have recently undergone a process of healing. Once the healing process is complete, the energy shall traverse the chakras unimpeded. You will come to the realization that they do not require any additional energy whatsoever. Consequently, this would entail the initiation of the proper rotational motion within the chakras. There exist numerous varied suppositions regarding the rotational patterns of the chakras. There is a prevailing belief that the chakras rotate in a clockwise manner, while an alternate perspective exists positing that the chakras rotate in a counterclockwise direction. It is advisable to consider the notion that your chakras exhibit clockwise rotation when in a state of equilibrium, and conversely, counter-clockwise rotation when experiencing an imbalance.

What are the distinct stages encompassing the chakra system?

The various stages of the chakra are perpetually determined by the encompassing energy within the chakras. Before delving into the various methods available to restore and harmonize the chakras for the promotion of overall well-being, it is paramount to familiarize oneself with the four crucial phases associated with this process.

Active Phase

The nomenclature of the phase accurately conveys its intended meaning. This is the ideal state for your chakra alignment. At this stage, your chakra is operating flawlessly. As an illustration, let us consider the root chakra. It has been conveyed to you that this particular chakra consistently assists in comprehending one's condition during instances of heightened stress or danger, such as those demanding a rapid response. When this operates efficiently, you will consistently have the ability to ensure your physical and mental well-being. The vibrancy of your Aura will perpetually remain illuminated when all the chakras are in this state.

Underactive Phase

This phase resembles the student who consistently maintains a solemn silence during class. He simply requires a stimulus to begin performing optimally within the educational setting. This chakra also necessitates a gentle nudge for its optimal functioning. When one encounters challenging circumstances, it becomes evident that this particular chakra has begun to function effectively. Regardless of whether the changes occur in the external environment or within your body, you will possess the capability to elicit a physiological response for self-preservation.

Passive Phase

This represents a period during which your body experiences tranquility and relaxation. This occurs when your chakra is in a state of rest as a result of achieving equilibrium in the energy within your body. This occurs when there is a constant state of equilibrium between the energy within your body and the energy surrounding it. This is analogous to solving a chemical equation on a Chemistry exam.

Overactive Phase

This phenomenon arises when one experiences intense emotional states.

You will observe that the vitality within the chakras exhibits a remarkable sensitivity to the stimuli present in the surrounding environment. It is possible that an abundance of energy may reside within these chakras, thus giving rise to imbalances of a physical and mental nature.

Restoring Equilibrium To The Throat Chakra

The fifth chakra is commonly referred to as the 'throat chakra' and is recognized as 'vishuddha' in the Sanskrit language. Located in the anterior region of the throat, possessing a vibrant hue of blue, intricately linked with the ethereal element, its emblematic representation can be observed hereunder:

What is the Function of the Throat Chakra?

The throat chakra, as its name implies, pertains to the region of your neck and encompasses your aptitude for expressing yourself articulately, assuredly, and truthfully. It influences your aptitude in verbal expression, as well as pertains to your commitment to veracity, integrity, adeptness in managing confrontations and disagreements, proficiency in active listening and effective communication, and proficiency in cultivating and maintaining interpersonal connections. Furthermore, it assumes responsibility for the functioning of your throat, neck, parathyroid and thyroid glands, oral cavity, larynx, and tongue, as well as any complications associated with these areas.

What Are the Consequences of Throat Chakra Blockage and How Does It Manifest When the Chakra is Attuned?

An efficiently operating throat chakra enables sincere and articulate communication, comfortable self-expression, effortless interaction with others, attentive listening, and effective fulfillment of personal requirements. Additionally, one experiences a sense of agency and mastery over oneself and one's own personal affairs. Furthermore, you scarcely encounter any health ailments associated with the aforementioned regions.

Notwithstanding the aforementioned, in instances where the throat chakra experiences obstruction, individuals encounter difficulties in effectively expressing themselves, exhibit an inability to communicate truthfully, face challenges in interpersonal communication, encounter obstacles in discerning their genuine needs, and contend with various manifestations such as discomfort in the neck area, irregularities in hormone levels, irritations in the throat, and complications related to oral hygiene. Let us examine the means by which you may eliminate these issues.

What are the Methods to Restore Harmony and Balance in the Throat Chakra?

"To alleviate imbalances in the throat chakra, consider implementing the following remedies:

Crystal Healing

Semiprecious stones of a blue hue are effective in harmonizing the energy associated with the throat chakra. Lapis Lazuli can be considered the optimal stone in that aspect. It is commonly known as the 'stone of truth', hence incorporating it into your daily routine aids in the balancing of your throat chakra, facilitating the expression of truth. Obtain an intricately crafted pendant from the material and tailor its length so that it consistently rests upon your neck, effectively dislodging any obstructions within the throat chakra caused by stagnant energies. Additionally, it is possible to utilize alternative gemstones like Turquoise, Amazonite, and Aquamarine in the shape of jewelry to harmonize and rebalance the fifth chakra, also known as the throat chakra. To alleviate impediments within the throat chakra, it is recommended to allocate 10 minutes of your daily routine to delicately hold your selected gemstone near your throat or engage in a gentle neck massage using the stone.

Meditative Practice

Please find a serene location and engage in deep breathing exercises for approximately 10 to 20 repetitions. It is essential that you maintain a breath retention within your thoracic region for a duration of 5 to 10 seconds, followed by a vigorous exhalation. This straightforward method effectively alleviates energy imbalances in the throat region.

Furthermore, gently close your eyes and proceed to inhale and exhale leisurely, encouraging a state of deep relaxation as you envision each muscle in your body gradually releasing tension in unison with each breath. Following a brief interval, envisage a gentle azure glow rotating seamlessly within the location of the throat chakra. Envision the intensification and expansion of its luminosity, synchronously growing with each inhalation, while gradually extending and encompassing your entire being.

Engage in this activity for a duration of 10 to 20 minutes, visualizing the gradual dissipation of any challenges pertaining to the throat chakra. By consistently engaging in this activity, within a few weeks, you will witness a remarkable enhancement in your ability to express candidly and effectively interact with individuals.

Consume Appropriate Nutritional Choices

It is essential to incorporate nourishing wholegrain foods, such as brown rice and whole-wheat grain, alongside tree-grown fruits like oranges, pears, and apples, as well as blue-hued foods like berries, into your dietary regimen. These specific food choices effectively alleviate any potential energy congestion within the throat chakra. In addition, incorporate spices such as ginger powder, cumin, and all-spices into your meals to promote balance in the throat chakra.

Affirmations

It is advised to recite the subsequent affirmations in a resolute manner as a means of restoring balance to your fifth chakra.

I express my emotions with ease and sincerity.

I effectively engage in impactful communication with others, compellingly persuading them.

I possess exceptional listening skills and excel in effective communication.

I communicate with compassion, integrity, and genuineness.

I have a natural aptitude for socializing and possess the ability to effortlessly engage and attract others.

Each time I engage in conversation, I maintain a poised and sincere demeanor.

While reciting these affirmations, envision yourself articulating with self-assurance and sincerity. To achieve optimal outcomes expeditiously, allocate 10 minutes twice a day for diligent practice. Now, let us proceed to the subsequent wherein we delve into the intricacies pertaining to the sixth chakra.

6: Optimal Chakra Functioning for Enhanced Well-being

An efficiently harmonized network of chakras can bring about remarkable benefits for your overall well-being, encompassing the realms of the mind, body, and spirit. If you identified considerable similarities between yourself and the content explored in three, it is highly probable that you have come to acknowledge the necessity of employing these strategies in order to enhance your alignment with your physical and spiritual existence. Could you please elaborate on the precise processes and effects that occur when one's chakras attain equilibrium? What immediate advantages will you experience upon embarking on this challenging yet highly rewarding regimen of existence?

Attaining equilibrium in your root chakra can significantly enhance your sense of self-assurance. As one applies rational thinking, the fear tends to diminish, facilitating a more balanced sleep pattern free from concerns surrounding monetary matters, job stability, mortgage obligations, and similar aspects. By reducing your concerns, you will experience an improvement in your well-being. You will experience the liberation of releasing grudges and anger, resulting in a state of tranquility and freedom. The resolution of financial challenges will occur autonomously, and there is potential for an increase in monetary gains beyond the initial state. Additionally, your body weight will reach a stable equilibrium, wherein individuals who are underweight will experience weight gain, and those who are overweight will undergo weight loss, resulting in improved well-being and appearance. This will contribute to the amelioration of physical ailments such as fluctuations in blood sugar levels and chronic conditions like diabetes.

The optimal functioning of the sacral chakra will facilitate artistic flourishing. Engaging in these activities will foster increased creative expression and a desire to participate in physical pursuits. You'll feel less inhibited and find much more pleasure in sex. If you are experiencing addictive sexual behavior, restoring balance to this chakra will provide an opportunity to cultivate a wholesome and fulfilling sexual life, where you can experience fulfillment and spiritual enrichment through intimate connections with your partner. You will experience a heightened sense of openness and increased freedom. Infections affecting the genital area will resolve, along with alleviation of discomfort in the kidneys and liver. Your bladder will be devoid of infections and the alleviation of back pain will be experienced.

When the warrior chakra attains equilibrium, you will possess the capability to accomplish all your desires. Unexpected avenues of opportunity will unveil themselves, surpassing your initial expectations. You will inevitably materialize precisely the things you desire, devoid of any undesired circumstances. You will experience a sense of self-assurance, tranquility in your environment, and exhibit remarkable self-control, enabling you to achieve your aspirations. Your emotional wellbeing will remain robust and harmonious, enabling you to provide assistance to others just as you have aided yourself, devoid of any adverse sentiments towards them. When the balance of this chakra is restored, ailments related to digestion, including those pertaining to the spleen, stomach, and gallbladder, will cease to persist.

By attaining a state of equilibrium within the heart chakra, one can achieve emotional mastery. One will experience feelings of empathy and possess a desire to assist others. You will emanate boundless affection and embrace, while maintaining appropriate boundaries to ensure that harm from others is not tolerated. You shall cultivate resilience and assertiveness in your romantic endeavors, while maintaining a healthy balance of influence without veering into manipulative or domineering behavior. Indeed, you will serve as a pillar of fortitude for others, whom they will admire and depend on. Unsightly emotions will dissipate from your being, enabling you to conquer feelings of envy and self-doubt and embrace both yourself and others unconditionally. Enhancement of blood circulation, stabilization of blood pressure, and potential amelioration of cardiac and respiratory ailments can be achieved by attaining equilibrium in this particular chakra. Furthermore, it will assist in alleviating symptoms of anxiety and depression.

An optimized state of the throat chakra will facilitate the complete and uninhibited articulation of one's thoughts and emotions. You will gain a genuine understanding of your rightful position within society and be able to manifest it in a positive and constructive manner. Your ability to communicate will enhance, leading to a greater sense of self-expression. One may experience an increased inclination towards laughter, a heightened frequency of smiles, and an overall elevated state of happiness. You will enhance your clarity of communication and convey your thoughts with compassion and benevolence, devoid of any form of prejudice or conceit. Individuals are inclined to engage in conversation and entrust in you to a greater extent, while your remarkable personal aura attracts others towards you. Lymphatic issues will resolve, thereby reducing susceptibility to oral cavity and oropharyngeal malignancies, as well as dental caries. Instances of otalgia and sinusitis will abate.

When the equilibrium of your third eye chakra is maintained, your perception will extend beyond mere visual input and enable you to perceive with unparalleled clarity. Your discernment will remain unclouded, and your intuition will prove accurate. One can discern falsehoods and unravel hidden motives by intuitively perceiving others, an immensely advantageous talent that proves beneficial across various circumstances. When the equilibrium of your third eye chakra is restored, your pineal gland will be in a state of good health, facilitating a heightened spiritual connection and, consequently, contributing to the harmonization of your crown chakra. Through the attainment of a harmoniously balanced throat chakra, the clarity and depth of your dreams will be enhanced, potentially leading to phenomena such as prophetic dreaming, lucid dreaming, and in extraordinary instances, telepathy, all of which are unattainable without the proper alignment of this vital energetic center. When this particular chakra achieves equilibrium, it is likely that your complexion will become clearer. The discomfort of headaches shall subside, and your body shall generate an ample quantity of melatonin, facilitating a restful and rejuvenating sleep experience.

A well-aligned crown chakra facilitates a connection to the spiritual realm and nurtures a deep understanding of one's position in both the spiritual and physical planes. When the crown chakra is in a state of equilibrium, your intuitive abilities will be heightened and precise. You shall experience a life devoid of apprehension, and place unwavering faith in the cosmic powers to provide assistance and solace. You, conversely, will be inclined to achieve a state of unity with those forces, thereby attaining a state of tranquility. Your feelings of anxiety, anger, and depression will dissipate. Attaining equilibrium in this particular chakra can yield a potent impact in the realm of healing, serving to mitigate and forestall conditions such as schizophrenia. Furthermore, it possesses the potential to act as a preventative measure against ailments such as Parkinson's disease and Alzheimer's disease. Individuals who are afflicted by seizures may find solace through the utilization of crown chakra healing techniques.

Achieving optimal well-being of the mind, body, and spirit necessitates the establishment of a harmonized and equilibrated network of chakras. Certain individuals go through life without encountering any disturbances in their chakras, while the majority of individuals are likely to experience concerns with their chakras at some juncture in their lives. Hence, it is crucial to commence these practices at present and strive to achieve mastery of your system with expediency. Our skin, eyes, and faces clear up and light up when our chakras are balanced; we are generally more physically healthy from exercise and yoga and more spiritually fit from meditation. The chakra diet enhances our metabolism's efficiency, resulting in the elimination of many illnesses or the relief of their symptoms. The dynamic equilibrium and harmonious circulation of energy within our physiological systems contribute to our overall well-being, promoting happiness, vitality, and cleanliness.

3:
Chakra Awareness

Having acquired knowledge about the different types of Chakra within the 7 Chakras system, it is evident that the

Chakras not only possess the ability to absorb energy, but also emit vibrational energy and exert influence over significant organs or glands that are interconnected with other bodily functions. Prior to harnessing the potential of your Chakras, it is essential to identify the specific Chakra upon which you intend to focus your efforts for enhancement. You have the option to enhance them collectively, however, in the case of individuals new to the concept of Chakras, it is advisable to dissect and prioritize the specific symptoms they aim to address first. It bears resemblance to the cultivation of consciousness pertaining to the presence of Chakras within oneself. Having well-balanced and harmonized Chakras will lead to increased happiness and a heightened sense of self-awareness.

Conversely, in the event that your Chakras are imbalanced, you will experience a persistent sense of stagnation, a profound melancholy, or a pervasive lack of direction in your existence. If a Chakra center becomes desynchronized from the rainbow chain, there is a potential for subsequent disruption in the connected organs and glands, likely resulting in the subsequent desynchronization of the nearest Chakras. However, once you successfully maintain the connection of these Chakras with their respective energy channels, you will attain favorable outcomes and experience a state of profound contentment.

In order to cultivate an understanding and facilitate the activation of these Chakras within oneself, it is essential to recognize that there exist solely three states associated with these energy centers: harmoniously balanced and receptive Chakras, imbalanced or obstructed Chakras. In conclusion, the hyperactive Chakras can be characterized as an excessively stimulated condition. Each individual Chakra possesses its unique method of achieving equilibrium and expansiveness. The obstruction occurs due to either a lack of awareness in your body or engaging in activities that have resulted in its closure.

Through the 7 main types of Chakras in its system, you can see that they are chained in the straight rainbow line, and each of them represents the core of your body. It is crucial to acknowledge that the Chakras reside within one's physical being and any actions undertaken possess the potential to impact them. Consequently, they will similarly exert influence on your life, potentially either adversely or positively.

Furthermore, as previously stated in regard to Universal energy, it applies uniformly to all Chakras. You aspire to channel this divine essence within your being and derive its advantageous outcomes through the pursuit of Chakra equilibrium. Indeed, the pursuit of tranquility of mind and vitality of the physical self is a universal aspiration.

This is the provision afforded by the Chakra energy. It evokes the omnipresent energy that envelops us, enabling us to appreciate the serenity inherent in our natural existence. We will now proceed to examine the three states of Chakras in order to enhance your understanding and facilitate your exploration of these Chakras.

Balancing

It is a frequent occurrence for individuals to inquire about techniques for harmonizing their Chakras. In order to prevent any depletion or inefficiency of energy, it is imperative that the harmonized energies establish and sustain an uninterrupted channel of circulation within the body. It is an influential cycle that necessitates iteration, commencing from the initial Chakra known as the Root Chakra, progressing upward to the pinnacle, referred to as the Crown Chakra.

When the Chakras are in proper alignment, we experience a state of profound energetic cohesion, enabling us to attain clarity regarding our life's purpose. To uphold a suitable equilibrium within these Chakras, it is imperative to comprehend the condition of one's intellect, essence, and physique. Examples of inquiries include the duration for which you are able to maintain a stationary position, your preferred hue, your pastimes, elements that elicit joy and discontent, and, crucially, comprehending your personal requirements. These matters hold significant importance in the process of self-discovery.

In addition to the aforementioned techniques, alternative means of facilitating the constructive flow of these energies encompass practices such as engaging in Yoga, partaking in meditative sessions, engaging in physical exercise, and cultivating vegetation. Additionally, engaging in acts of kindness and promoting virtuous actions is the optimal means to nurture your Chakras and maintain your overall well-being. Maintaining equilibrium in your Chakras will aid in alleviating any imbalance that may deplete your energy. It has the potential to mitigate the hyperactive state of Chakras before it deteriorates further. As a result, it is imperative to achieve equilibrium within your Chakras by attuning to them and removing any surplus energies within each Chakra. This process facilitates the cultivation of a positive mindset, spiritual connectivity, and physical well-being.

9 – Eminent Individuals Who Embrace the Chakra System

The Chakra System may be perceived as a highly mystical subject, however, it should be noted that numerous esteemed individuals within the scientific community have expressed favorable opinions regarding its validity. Acquiring insight into their perspectives will not only bolster your conviction in the existence of energy centers, but it will also enhance your understanding of the human condition.

Carl Gustav Jung, a renowned Swiss psychiatrist and psychotherapist, gained recognition for his significant contributions to the field of analytical psychiatry. Initially a fervent adherent of Freudian theory, he eventually embraced the integration of Kundalini Yoga and Chakras into the realm of Psychology. He was among the initial psychologists who integrated both yoga and chakra into the Western hemisphere.

In contrast to his contemporaries, Mr. Jung regarded the unconscious as an authentic entity and adamantly maintained that to comprehend one's unconscious, it is imperative to delve further into one's own distinctiveness. Initially, he regarded Chakras as representations, positing that the deeper one's self-awareness, the more profound the reverence for these symbolic elements.

Consider the ROOT CHAKRA as an illustrative instance. According to Carl Jung, this symbol represents our limited knowledge confined solely to the external world. By cultivating and enhancing this chakra, we attain a heightened awareness of occurrences within the corporeal realm. If a person moves up, that is, he begins to encounter the SACRAL CHAKRA, and then he is "baptized" for the unconscious realm. At that juncture, he not only acquires knowledge of the tangible realm, but embarks on a transformative odyssey towards the enigmatic depths of the unconscious mind. Upon reaching the Third Chakra, commonly known as the Solar Plexus, an individual undergoes a significant transformation akin to a rebirth, as they become aware of and must confront a range of emotions and sensations that were previously unfamiliar to them. Upon reaching the HEART CHAKRA, individuals will gain the capacity to contemplate their emotions rather than solely focusing on physical sensations. Put simply, the individual will possess the ability to dissociate from their emotions. The apex resides within the throat energy center, known as the chakra. Upon attaining this symbol, an individual's realm transcends the confines of the physical dimension and extends into the depths of their inner psyche. It is of utmost significance to acknowledge that according to Carl Jung's perspective, the attainment of the 6th and 7th chakras was considered unattainable by individuals. According to his explanation, the THIRD EYE Chakra signifies the convergence of an individual's inner essence with the divine realm. The notion of THE CROWN is beyond his comprehension.

Despite the pronounced divergence between Carl Jung's perspectives and Eastern concepts, it cannot be disputed that his substantial contributions have had a profound impact on the assimilation of the Chakra System within Western discourse.

Nikola Tesla, a renowned electrical engineer and inventor, drew inspiration from Vedic Philosophy, a philosophical tradition that posits the interconnectedness and dynamism of all phenomena. In accordance with the principles outlined in the Vedic texts, it is posited that tangible matter originates from an initial substance or ethereal essence, surpassing the limits of human comprehension. This substance, known as the akasha or luminiferous ether, permeates all space and is subject to the influence of the animating energy known as prana or the creative force. This primal force continually instigates the emergence of all entities and phenomena in perpetually recurring cycles. The Sanskrit terms 'prana' and 'akash' serve as linguistic representations of matter and force within the Vedic scriptures.

Given the abundance of resources accessible on the internet, it would be prudent to gather a variety of references and diligently peruse them individually. It may come as a surprise to discover that familiarizing oneself with the chakra system can also serve as a means to enhance one's understanding of oneself.

Meditation And Yoga

Within this chapter, we shall delve into the chronicles of meditation and its profound potential to purify one's mind, body, and spirit. There exists a multitude of diverse meditation practices available for your engagement, which shall not solely bestow clarity and serenity into your existence, but also foster equilibrium within your chakral system. Throughout the course of this book, we have explored the concept of meditation as a means of achieving equilibrium and unblocking your chakras. However, we now intend to delve deeper into this topic, aiming to provide you with a comprehensive comprehension of the profound significance of this practice within your repertoire.

In addition, a concise overview of the historical background of Yoga will be provided, highlighting its potential benefits in various aspects of life, including its effects on one's chakras. We will allocate a brief period for the discussion of Yoga, as we have at your disposal another book that delves extensively into the subject, providing you with a comprehensive understanding and fostering a solid groundwork in this discipline. It is crucial that you comprehend the fundamental aspect that Yoga significantly influences your chakra system.

Meditation History

Meditation originates from the Latin term 'meditatum', which conveys the notion of deep contemplation. When individuals engage in the practice of meditation, they seek to establish a more tangible rapport with their inner selves as well as the external environment. It enables us to embrace and fully engage with the daily occurrences that unfold in our midst, rather than merely allowing them to slip away unnoticed. It fosters consciousness and enhances our emotional attunement.

The inquiry concerning the historical origin of meditation poses a challenge in providing a definitive response. Frankly speaking, it has existed for a considerable duration. Irrespective of the geographical region being studied, it can be observed that meditation pervades various cultures across the globe. A selection of the earliest iterations has been discovered in China and India, nevertheless, its utilization has been observed worldwide for successive generations.

The foundations of meditation can be traced back to the ancient texts derived from the customs and practices of the Hindu community. It was an integral aspect of the philosophical framework embraced by the institution and held in high regard as a means of attaining spiritual illumination. The precise origins of meditation have undergone extensive deliberation over a considerably protracted period, leaving the likelihood of definitively pinpointing its inception rather elusive.

Meditation is highly prevalent in contemporary society, and it is widely recognized that its origins predate the advent of written language. Similar to all phenomena, meditation has undergone adaptations over the course of its existence. The diversity of meditation practices may vary significantly based on one's cultural background and geographical location. Studying the historical origins and foundations of diverse cultures can contribute to the expansion of your understanding of this time-honored tradition.

Before the advent of written records, depictions of meditation images were found in the form of wall art. They depict individuals assuming meditative positions, exhibiting an apparent state of genuine serenity and relaxation. These paintings are located in India. or These paintings can be found in India. or India is the original source of these paintings.

Hindu customs shed light on the prevalence of cave meditation among the yogis of that era. It is imperative to acknowledge that a significant number of contemporary meditation traditions have derived from this lineage of practices. This encompasses the utilization of movement techniques derived from the principles and traditions of Hatha Yoga. These Yoga practices deviate significantly from contemporary perceptions, encompassing a distinct repertoire of movements and cognitive frameworks. It has undergone significant development over the course of time.

The practice of meditation is intrinsically linked to the teachings of Buddhism. The majority of portrayals depicting the Buddha showcase him in a serene meditative posture. In the Buddhist lexicon, the term meditation is effectively referred to as "bahavana", conveying the concept of attaining a state of mental tranquility. The principles and techniques of Buddhist meditation greatly diverge from those of other traditions. As their progress was unfolding, so too were their counterparts in regions such as India, China, and various other parts of the world. Although their primary objectives revolve around clarity and tranquility, there were differences in the teachings and practices among them.

Meditation did not emerge in the Western world until around the 1700s.

The methods of meditation and their associated practices were translated into various languages through the interpretation of philosophical literature. After the translations meditation was typically a simple discussion between intellectuals. In the approximately 20th century, it gained greater prominence as an actual application rather than merely an object of discourse.

In the late 1960s, there was a notable shift wherein the exploration of meditation primarily began to focus on psychological outcomes, resulting in a significant detachment of spirituality from this practice. The practice of meditation has been reported to effectively alleviate stress, enhance mindfulness, and significantly contribute to resolving detrimental aspects in an individual's life. As this information became increasingly known, individuals began embracing the principles of meditation.

As time progressed, the component of mindfulness in meditation became integrated with a diverse range of therapeutic modalities, including cognitive-behavioral therapy. The results were amazing. The growing number of individuals embracing meditation can be attributed to the remarkable outcomes experienced by practitioners.

In contemporary times, meditation has gained global recognition and has become a prevalent practice among a multitude of individuals. Irrespective of one's social standing, meditation can prove to be beneficial. Given its undeniable impact on countless individuals, it comes as no surprise that it has garnered such widespread acclaim. Although meditation may lack empirical evidence, its efficacy will become evident through observable outcomes.

The practice of meditation possesses the capacity to enhance the lives of individuals in a vast array of manners. Certain individuals have reported that it has the potential to alleviate sensations of pain, alleviate stress and alleviate sensations of anxiety. It possesses the potential to enhance cardiovascular health and elevate the body's immune function. The practice of meditation facilitates a state of tranquility, which in turn confers numerous benefits upon us. It facilitates the liberation of our psyche and physique from any burdens that may be preoccupying us.

In the reverential linguistic tradition of Buddhism, the term Chakra (alternatively known as cakra) corresponds to the Sanskrit nomenclature denoting a circular object. The chakras are circular or disc-shaped sources of energy that reside within our subtle body, also referred to as our ethereal body.

Contemporary scientific inquiry has corroborated the notions postulated by esteemed philosophers such as Socrates, as well as the venerable ancient Rishis of India, by establishing that our essence transcends physical substance and is fundamentally constituted by energy. Quantum physics has provided evidence to support the notion that as one delves further into the atom, the extent of its existence diminishes. In the grand scheme of things, there exists solely a complex network of energetic dynamics. Atoms are remarkable diminutive entities that exhibit magnetic properties akin to mirrors, effectively assimilating and refracting light in an incessant manner. This event is responsible for the formation of our pigment. This phenomenon presents a perpetual cycle of energy expansion, rejuvenation, and reutilization.

In the midst of our daily routines, it is often overlooked that our physical beings are remarkable conduits that transport us. Permitting us to engage in dancing, physical contact, sensory perception, visual observation, and auditory perception. We are not solely corporeal entities, but rather expansive reservoirs of energy. When the term "ethereal body" or "subtle body" is encountered, it refers to the flow of energy that constitutes the fundamental essence of an individual.
us

in its most unadulterated state. Contemporary physiology indicates that these seven chakras exhibit precise alignment with our primary nerve ganglia, tracing the course of the spinal column.

There exist seven primary chakra wheels that possess limitless energy vortexes, with each wheel interdependent upon and influencing various spheres of our existence. In ancient literature, particularly the texts pertaining to chakras (also known as cakra), one can find references to supplementary sub-chakras (cakra) such as Kalpataru, the celestial tree symbolizing desires within the heart chakra, or the Soma Chakra, positioned slightly above the Third Eye Chakra.

When our chakras are in a state of optimal well-being, their motion exhibits seamless fluidity and vibrant liveliness. Similar to our comprehension of our physical well-being, in a state of good health, we experience a sense of vitality, enhanced sensory perception, increased contentment, and a general sense of positive progression in life. The alleviation of stress is facilitated when we also experience physical well-being, resulting in its gradual dissipation at the conclusion of the day. This phenomenon takes place when your chakras are unobstructed and harmoniously aligned, enabling the untamed and unhindered flow of electrical energy to emanate.

The contrasting extremity of this spectrum is a concept that is universally recognized by individuals at varying points in their lives—poor health. This unfortunate condition manifests itself through the manifestation of illnesses, viruses, chronic ailments, and varying degrees of fatigue. Overall, we express discontent; perhaps our emotional sensitivity and melancholy are heightened, and our anxiety levels are elevated to an extreme intensity. Sudden and unanticipated sadness has the capacity to emerge and emotionally incapacitate us. Frequently, our dispositions exhibit a tendency to quickly ignite, leading us to develop feelings of upset and anger towards those in our immediate circle without substantial cause, thereby hasty overreactions come into play. This phenomenon can often occur in diverse manifestations and intensities when our chakras become congested and obstructed, leading to an imbalanced state. In brief, we descend into a state of misery. In addition to our declining health, we find ourselves constantly being hindered by the adversities that life presents.

I presume that you are currently contemplating the notion that chakras are not causing you distress.

The setting in which I operate professionally" or "The atmosphere in which I conduct my work It is plausible that you may be correct to a certain degree; nevertheless, it is important to bear in mind that our incorporeal essence operates much akin to our corporeal form. Consuming improperly cooked or excessively aged chicken results in illness. External factors perpetually influence individuals in various aspects. Harmful substances present in the atmosphere, as well as radiation emitted by the everyday electronics we rely on, possess the potential to induce ailments in the human body, consequently impacting the well-being of our chakras.

The harmonious equilibrium between physical, emotional, and energetic well-being plays a pivotal role in the attainment of happiness and optimal health. Like we take vitamins and minerals, eat well, and exercise to keep our physical bodies as healthy as possible we have the same ability to care for our chakras that we have to care for our whole self.

Four: Harnessing the Power of the Solar Plexus Chakra - Manipura

The third chakra is known as the solar plexus or navel chakra, alternatively referred to as "Manipura" in Sanskrit, signifying the meaning of "City of The Shining Jewel." The auditory impression produced by this particular object is a resonant "ram". It is associated with the sense of sight and is situated in the vicinity of the navel. It emits a yellow luminescence and serves as a dwelling for the embodiment of the fiery element. The gland in question refers to the pancreas.

The central essence of the matter revolves around the acquisition and exertion of authority. Manipura serves as a catalyst for attaining self-control and enables us to assume responsibility for our lives and destinies. The pursuit of a prosperous professional life and the harmonious management of a well-functioning household are under the influence of the third chakra. This chakra holds great importance for certain spiritual traditions due to the abundance of energy it possesses.

In Ayurveda, a time-honored medical practice in India that is closely aligned with yoga, it is believed that the majority of ailments can be effectively treated by restoring equilibrium to the digestive system and fostering optimal digestive metabolism. Similarly, harmonizing this chakra brings about automatic resolution of issues in various domains, making it a recommended initial measure to undertake in the pursuit of healing. A robust central foundation translates into resolute determination, unwavering confidence, and unwieldy strength—conversely, individuals with an asymmetrical core are prone to experiencing a sense of powerlessness or may develop domineering tendencies.

It has been purported that achieving equilibrium in this realm enables the passage to boundless spiritual prosperity, and those who operate from this core possess an unblemished composure, resolute determination, and purposeful conduct. In Zen philosophy, the concept analogous to the navel is referred to as the "hara". The Zen meditator focuses on the hara to provide mental stability and clear the mind as upper centers are accessed.

The energy center in the abdomen holds great significance in both Zen and qi gong traditions, as it is believed to encapsulate a miniature representation of the cosmos. In the past few years, a substantial body of research has emerged regarding the profound importance and cognitive capacities residing within the abdominal region. This area is home to a majority of our immune cells and has been characterized as our secondary neurological center. "Gut" reactions represent the innate intuitive intelligence that resides within our being. It is hardly surprising that contemporary scientific research is increasingly substantiating assertions made in ancient civilizations.

During adolescence, the core issues tend to be most apparent for the majority of individuals. Adolescence constitutes the period characterized by the shift from childhood to adulthood. It is a period wherein individuals must develop self-reliance, exercise autonomous decision-making, and assume mastery over their own existence. This is evident in various relational, educational, and occupational contexts. Unless adolescents acquire the ability to harness their own potential and take charge of their direction, achieving success will remain elusive. As they are granted increased liberties, their learning is enhanced in tandem with the accumulation of additional duties to bear in mind.

When young individuals successfully acquire proficiency in these tasks, they experience a sense of capability and self-assurance. They discover their areas of proficiency and determine how to leverage their capabilities in a productive manner. Notwithstanding, it is widely recognized that adolescence is often characterized by considerable unrest. The task of cultivating naval energy proves to be challenging, and assuming the responsibility and obligation of being in control can prove to be a daunting and intimidating prospect for numerous individuals. Individuals who are unable to cultivate a foundation of fundamental vitality may exhibit aggressive tendencies towards others or engage in behaviors that are detrimental to themselves, both during adolescence and in subsequent stages of life.

Of course, the functioning of the digestive system is governed by Manipura. The small intestine, liver, and autonomic nervous system are likewise affected. Indications of an imbalance in the region include, but are not limited to, digestive disorders, hepatic insufficiency, diminished vitality, disordered eating habits, diabetes, middle back weakness, musculoskeletal rigidity, and compromised posture.

Furthermore, the naval region predominantly revolves around the notion of authority, and indications of inadequate power in this area manifest through emotional symptoms such as diminished self-confidence, compromised determination, consistent inability to attain objectives, and the inclination to shift accountability onto others rather than acknowledging personal shortcomings. When one's intrinsic motivation is depleted, achieving success appears exceedingly difficult, prompting individuals to seek validation from others and assume a more submissive demeanor. The experience of solitude can evoke fear, while the act of protecting ourselves poses challenges, and we are susceptible to crumbling in the face of external judgments and behaviors.

While individuals with a diminished core display a tendency to diminish in size, those exhibiting excessive activation of the naval chakra exhibit heightened aggression and an overwhelming tendency towards expansion. Exhibiting excessive competitiveness, bullying behavior, domineering tendencies, extreme anger, and a narcissistic disposition are characteristics that suggest an individual's lack of emotional equilibrium. Furthermore, the adverse consequences of an excessive amount of energy in this domain are noteworthy.

These include the generation of excessive heat, which may give rise to muscular contractions, gastric ulcers, heightened stress levels, and insatiable appetite. These conceited and ambitious individuals may exhibit traits of workaholism, and develop an unhealthy preoccupation with achieving success and exerting control. When individuals experience a developmental stagnation within this specific chakra, they tend to become fixated on exerting control over their surroundings.

Nevertheless, the central area exhibits decreased activity in the majority of individuals, with only a limited few possessing a well-balanced and robust abdominal region. Individuals who perceive themselves to lack control and face a sense of unaccomplishment will greatly advantage from engaging in core exercises. Similarly, the manifestation of Manipura weakness can be observed through adverse responses like unbecoming envy, bellicosity, and a lack of capacity to withstand constructive criticism. Stomach discomfort and comparable indications are warning signs to be vigilant about.

Once the equilibrium of energy is achieved, a sense of certainty and security permeates your being. Assuredness is effortlessly attained while uncertainties dissipate. It signifies displaying resilience and competence while upholding the fundamental rights of others. Authentic power is never assertive; rather, it manifests itself through individuals who possess remarkable strength internally while exhibiting a quiet and conscientious demeanor. Such individuals garner immediate respect from others (or are met with resentment from individuals struggling with their own personal conflicts), without resorting to overt actions to elicit such a response.

Difficulties are faced with composure and a constructive mindset, and barriers are never sidestepped. Employment holds significant value, yet it should not overwhelm one's existence, typically demonstrating a degree of selflessness. The person possesses a highly efficient moral compass and exhibits unwavering dedication towards their vocation. Their vitality is exceptional, and their sense of purpose is unwavering.

The individual exhibiting traits of the navel chakra personality is known for their exceptional inner strength and unwavering determination. These individuals are the catalysts of progress and catalysts of change. Their capacity to attain success can often appear extraordinarily supernatural. Manipura possesses an abundance of vital energy, leading these individuals to display heightened sensitivity towards the needs of others and demonstrate benevolence in their intentions. Numerous individuals who possessed great wisdom and insight in their early years were predominantly introspective, with their strong focus on self-exploration often fueling a deep longing for spiritual growth.

When in a state of equilibrium, they exhibit accomplishment, determination, influence, and a strong focus on objectives. They conduct themselves with dual consideration, both for their personal benefit and the well-being of others, while judiciously employing their inherent sensitivity and empathy. As previously indicated, though, individuals with this particular personality disposition may become excessively preoccupied with striving for influence and authority. Their primary source of apprehension stems from relinquishing control, and they stand to gain significant advantages by acquiring the skill of letting go and calming their minds. The larynx, which primarily governs both verbal and non-verbal expression, serves to harmonize the innate energy emanating from the abdomen, thus achieving a state of equilibrium within the individual. A robust spirit is equally imperative when authority assumes a pivotal role in one's existence.

Physical activities such as pilates, which target the abdominal muscles, are beneficial for the Manipura chakra. Abdominal manipulation and controlled respiratory techniques, such as kapalabhati, serve to induce stimulation in the abdominal region, facilitating the restoration of chakra equilibrium. Twists serve as highly beneficial exercises for the digestive system, owing to their capacity to compress and extract impurities from the region, while also facilitating the flow of revitalizing energy.

Consuming easily digestible foods, along with enhancing overall digestion, is advantageous. This includes engaging in cleanses, periods of fasting, and incorporating probiotics or digestive enzymes. Incorporating mustard tones into your attire and establishing a harmonious resonance with the element of fire are equally efficacious measures. Certain individuals may opt to engage in reflective meditation, directing their focus towards a flickering flame. Developing the ability to heed one's intuition is crucial. Learning to be courageous and resolute in one's daily endeavors is of utmost importance. Frequently, the ability to reach a decision holds greater significance than the decision itself.

Citrine, pyrite, tiger's eye, and amber, which belong to the spectrum of yellow and gold stones, are deemed suitable for placement on the naval area. Lavender, lemon, and anise essential oils also possess advantageous properties. Fennel, chamomile, and juniper possess beneficial properties, and anise and cardamom are apt seasonings to incorporate into your culinary regimen. The metallic composition is comprised of the element mercury, while the resonant nature of musical string instruments, such as the violin, bestows energy upon the lotus.

Evacuating the gastrointestinal tract is an excellent technique to restore equilibrium to your abdominal region. There exist numerous fasting and detoxification programs, and certain ones necessitate the supervision of a qualified specialist. One activity that can be undertaken within the confines of one's residence is engaging in an Ayurvedic kitchari cleanse. Kitchari is a traditional Indian culinary creation that is suitable for consumption as part of a dietary purification regimen. Due to its elevated protein content and favorable digestive properties, this dietary approach permits the body to undergo a cleansing process without resorting to fasting, thereby affording the digestive system an opportunity to recuperate and reenergize. The meal consists of a combination of lentils, rice, assorted spices, and clarified butter, with the possibility of incorporating vegetables as an optional component. It possesses tridoshic properties, rendering it suitable for individuals of all constitutions while providing exceptional nutritional value.

Mono-diet cleanses typically span a duration of approximately 10 days, although they can be tailored to be as short as three. Allocate a number of consecutive days during which minimal disruptions are anticipated, and ensure ample opportunity for repose. Consume kitchari as a substitute for your regular meals (oatmeal can be consumed for breakfast as an alternative). It is possible to prepare all the meals for the day in the morning, however, it is advisable to refrain from consuming leftovers and refrain from eating beyond 7 pm. Drink plenty of water. In addition to their beneficial properties, herbal teas and the herb triphala can also provide assistance. However, it is important to note that the process of cleansing is not recommended for women who are menstruating, pregnant, or currently breastfeeding. It is also advisable to refrain from engaging in such activities if you suffer from severe debility and infirmity.

www.ingramcontent.com/pod-product-compliance
Lightning Source LLC
Chambersburg PA
CBHW050235120526
44590CB00016B/2102